VOCABULARY SLEUTHS
Problem Solving With Words
Grades 5-7 Book 1

by
George Moore

World Teachers Press®

Published with the permission of R.I.C. Publications Pty. Ltd.

Copyright © 1999 by Didax, Inc., Rowley, MA 01969. All rights reserved.

First published by R.I.C. Publications Pty. Ltd., Perth, Western Australia.

Limited reproduction permission: The publisher grants permission to individual teachers who have purchased this book to reproduce the blackline masters as needed for use with their own students. Reproduction for an entire school or school district or for commercial use is prohibited.

Printed in the United States of America.

Order Number 2-5118
ISBN 1-58324-040-3

A B C D E F 03 02 01 00 99

395 Main Street
Rowley, MA 01969
www.worldteacherspress.com

Foreword

Vocabulary Sleuths is a series of two books developed to assist you with developing the vocabulary of your students. These innovative and fascinating activities have been classroom tested. The blackline masters have been designed to engage students in language development by introducing new words and expanding upon the meanings and usage of the vocabulary your students bring to the classroom.

This series has been designed for upper primary through early high school students. To stimulate the interest of your students these reproducible pages use a variety of innovative and creative word games and searches. The stimulating activities are designed to teach parts of speech, word derivations and some of the interesting ways in which words are used, whether written or spoken.

Each activity begins with a brief explanation of the concept being presented. Students should be encouraged to use a dictionary and/or a thesaurus whenever they find themselves stumped for an answer.

These books will help your students to develop a lifelong interest in words, their meanings and their usage. They will also assist them in becoming competent speakers and writers.

Contents	Page(s)
Teacher Information	4-5
Alphabetical Order 1	6
Alphabetical Order 2	7
Alphabetical Order 3	8
Word Families	9
Affixes	10
Bigger Than	11
Idioms	12
Colorful Language!	13
Missing Numbers	14
Occupations	15
Word Squares	16
Word Target 1	17
Word Target 2	18
Limericks	19
Adjectives	20
Crossword Puzzle - Similes	21
Anagram Verbs	22
Alliteration	23
Similies - Alliteration	24
Reordering Sentences	25

Contents	Page(s)
Jumbled Sentences	26
Homophones	27
Homonyms	28
Anagrams	29
Derivations	30
Collective Nouns	31
Adjectives	32
Word Pyramids	33
Acrostic	34
Mis_ing Parts	35
Acrostic - World Rivers	36
Crossword Puzzle - Nouns	37
Fun Word Rhymes	38
Word Snake - Social Studies	39
"Let's go, man!"	40
Creatures and Their Homes	41
Collective Nouns	42
Oceans and Continents	43
Endangered Animals	44
Interesting Words	45
Answers	46-48

Teacher Information

Before beginning the activities in *Vocabulary Sleuths*, review dictionary and thesaurus skills. The activities in this book can be used in a variety of situations, including:

1. **Whole Class**
    - Select the concept you would like to focus on; for example, verbs.
    - Select the appropriate worksheet to develop this concept with your group.
    - Each learner will require their own copy of the worksheet.
    - As a group, discuss the explanation at the top of the page and examples.
    - Ensure each student is clear about what they need to do to complete the sheet accurately.

2. **Small Group**
    - Form a small group, of five or six, who are all having difficulty with the same concept.
    - Select the appropriate worksheet to develop this concept with your group.
    - Each learner will require their own copy of the worksheet.
    - As a group, discuss the explanation at the top of the page and examples.
    - Ensure each student is clear about what they need to do to complete the sheet accurately.

3. **Independently**
    - Select the appropriate worksheet to develop a specific concept with the student.
    - Discuss the explanation at the top of the page and examples.
    - Ensure each learner is clear about what they need to do to complete the sheet accurately.
    - The worksheet may be completed during the lesson, or the student may wish to complete the work at home as part of a program.

Strategies

The activities supplied within this book have been designed to provide learners with opportunities to develop and practice various learning strategies.

Vocabulary Sleuths encourages learners to:

- look for patterns
- break words into chunks
- develop dictionary skills
- develop an awareness of less common words
- play with and manipulate words to form new words
- learn to use a thesaurus
- develop problem solving skills in regards to language and its use
- use various resources to find information and to ascertain that information is correct
- to develop lateral thinking skills encouraging students to delve deeper into words.

Teacher Information – Sample Lesson Plan

The following is a sample lesson plan using one of the pages in this book. It demonstrates how the activity could be introduced, developed and extended.

Activity
Alphabetical Order 1: Page 6

Introductory Work
This activity focuses on ordering words alphabetically.

Using the Worksheet
This activity can be linked to other aspects of the English curriculum, including, grammar and spelling. While this is predominantly a problem solving activity, it reinforces the basic knowledge of alphabetical order. Discussion can be based on alphabetical order.

1. Discuss alphabetical order, using several examples. Read and explain instructions with the group.

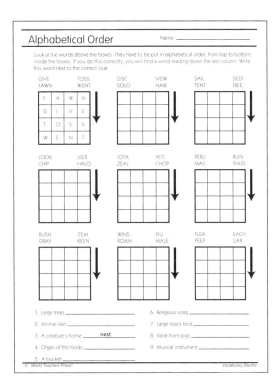

2. Complete the first examples with the group/individual using an overhead projector or enlarged copy of the worksheet.

3. Students work independently through the examples provided.

4. Students check their own work to ensure all their work is fully complete and accurate.

Extension
The extension of the activity is largely covered by following activities, however, further discussion and development of alphabetical order can occur if students are asked to extend the range of examples they already have.

Vocabulary Sleuths Book 1   World Teachers Press® 5

Alphabetical Order 1

Name: _____

Look at the words above the boxes. They have to be put in alphabetical order, from top to bottom, inside the boxes. If you do this correctly, you will find a word reading down the last column. Write this word next to the correct clue.

GIVE   TOSS
FAWN   WENT

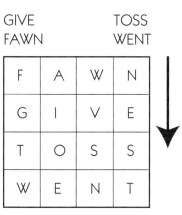

DISC   VIEW
SOLO   HAIR

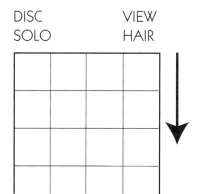

SAIL   DEEP
TENT   FREE

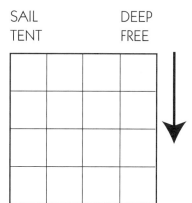

LOOK   JEER
CHIP   HALO

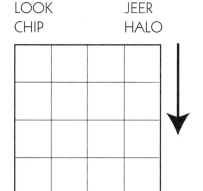

IOTA   YETI
ZEAL   CHOP

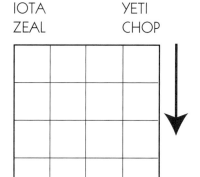

PERU   RUIN
MAIL   SNUG

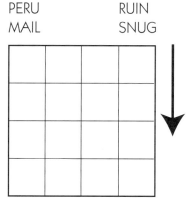

BUSH   ITEM
GRAY   KEEN

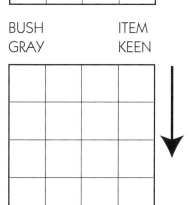

WINS   PILL
ROAM   MALE

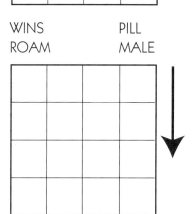

FLEA   EACH
PEEP   LIAR

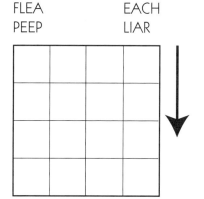

1. Large trees _____

2. Animal skin _____

3. A creature's home ___**nest**___

4. Organ of the body _____

5. A bucket _____

6. Religious song _____

7. Large black bird _____

8. Meat from pigs _____

9. Musical instrument _____

Alphabetical Order 2

Name: _____
(To second letter)

Look at the words above the boxes. They have to be put in alphabetical order, from top to bottom, inside the boxes.

If you do this correctly, you will find a word reading down the last column.
Write this word next to the correct clue below.

All the answers are **nouns** (names of things).

| PINE | PAIR |
| ROAD | RICE |

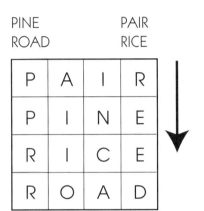

| PEAR | HERO |
| POND | HALF |

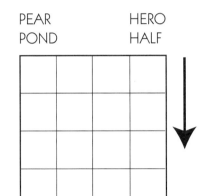

| BURN | COAT |
| BLOT | BONE |

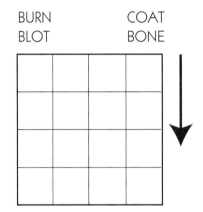

| VISA | CAMP |
| DOME | WINK |

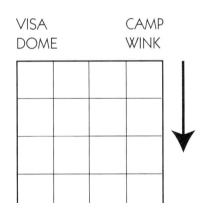

| TOGA | THIN |
| TWIT | SING |

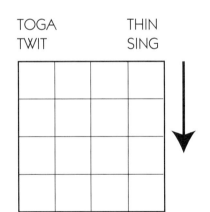

| LINE | LOAF |
| DASH | CHIC |

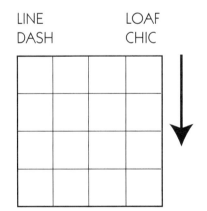

Before you put your answers in the correct place below, you need to check the word meanings in your dictionary.

1. A tiny insect _____

2. A mountain top _____

3. A water plant __**reed**_____

4. A shallow river crossing _____

5. A cook _____

6. Used when camping _____

Alphabetical Order 3

Name: _____

Look at the words above the boxes. They have to be put in alphabetical order from top to bottom inside the boxes. When this has been done, you will find a word reading down the last column. Place this word on the line below the correct clue at the bottom of the page.

melon	proud	manse	attic	cobra	blurb	cover	bough
blade	brawl	metal	llama	cater	dross	pinto	brake
delta		madam		dress		pylon	

B	L	A	D	E
B	R	A	W	L
D	E	L	T	A
M	E	L	O	N
P	R	O	U	D

voice	truce	undid	tunic	story	cramp	boast	beast
thumb	waist	twice	wafer	posts	mania	Balbo	rover
tutor		vista		plain		brave	

dingo	issue	brook	atlas	radii	rests	Cairo	blurb
isles	alarm	purse	pilot	pasta	radar	vices	throw
igloo		koala		cramp		towel	

wading bird | used for cereal | scented wood | capital of France

_____ | _____ | _____ | _____

flat, round hat | largest deer | African antelope | small flower
 | | **eland** |

_____ | _____ | _____ | _____

web-footed mammal | flat-bodied fish | a dromedary | mix of copper and zinc

Word Families

Name: _____
(Context clues)

In the boxes below are words which belong to the same family because they are alike in some way. Place the words on the correct line in the poem so the poem makes sense.

–ICK
stick quick trick
brick sick pick

–IGHT
slight night right
might fight light

He said his next _____

Was to swallow a _____

Yet in his throat it might _____

And make him so _____

That a doctor he'd _____

But he'd have to be _____ !

One dark cloudy _____

When there wasn't much _____

John started to _____

Though he was only _____

He fought with all his _____

But he knew it wasn't _____

–AIN
pain train drain
rain brain grain

–AKE
snake rake drake
lake quake brake

Joan fell down a _____

And this caused her some _____

So the girl used her _____

And she boarded a _____

But as it passed fields of _____

Down came the _____ !

Dad stepped on the _____

When a very large _____

Slid out of the _____

Though this made us _____

We chased it with a _____

But scared a duck and a _____

Check any word you don't know in your dictionary!

Vocabulary Sleuths Book 1   World Teachers Press® 9

Affixes

Name: _____

Syllables (or words) placed before or after words are called **affixes**. **Prefixes** are placed **before words**, while **suffixes** are placed at the **end of words**. Prefixes often come from French, Latin, or Greek and help us to understand the meanings of the words.

Prefixes

Place the list words beginning with **"tri"** (meaning "three") against the correct clues.

triangle	1.	**Three**-legged stand	_____
triplets	2.	Set of **three** plays or books	_____
trimaran	3.	Bicycle with **three** wheels	_____
tripod	4.	Spear with **three** prongs	_____
trident	5.	To cut into **three** parts	_____
trireme	6.	A flag with **three** stripes	_____
trilogy	7.	A **three**-sided shape	_____
trisect	8.	Roman ship with **three** sets of oars	_____
tricolor	9.	**Three** babies born at one time	_____
tricycle	10.	Ship with **three** hulls	_____

Suffixes

Select the correct suffix and place it at the **end** of each word. As you check the correct suffix in your dictionary, also check the word's meaning and place it under the correct clue.

–able	ign_____	notic_____	aud_____
–ible	ador_____	dirig_____	chang_____
–oble	ed_____	irasc_____	vis_____
–eable	peac_____	leg_____	mall_____

Clues

lovable	can be seen	dishonorable	airship
_____	_____	_____	_____
able to be read	not warlike	can be heard	can be eaten
_____	_____	_____	_____
easily seen	quick-tempered	can be altered	easily pressed into shape
_____	_____	_____	_____

Bigger Than

Name: _____
(Dictionary work)

Use the given words to fill in the gaps and make each sentence true.
Put your first two answers in alphabetical order.

Example:

cradle, bed, cot	A **bed** and a **cot** are bigger than a **cradle**
elephant, mouse, horse	An _____ and a _____ are bigger than a _____
squirrel, zebra, goat	A _____ and a _____ are bigger than a _____
mansion, cabin, palace	A _____ and a _____ are bigger than a _____
town, city, hamlet	A _____ and a _____ are bigger than a _____
pygmy, titan, ogre	An _____ and a _____ are bigger than a _____
iceberg, icicle, glacier	A _____ and an _____ are bigger than a _____
flower, wreath, bouquet	A _____ and a _____ are bigger than a _____
goose, wren, swan	A _____ and a _____ are bigger than a _____
seed, seedling, sapling	A _____ and a _____ are bigger than a _____
flea, locust, gnat	A _____ and a _____ are bigger than a _____
dolphin, sardine, herring	A _____ and a _____ are bigger than a _____
grape, peach, apricot	An _____ and a _____ are bigger than a _____
pelican, albatross, robin	An _____ and a _____ are bigger than a _____
beret, cloak, cardigan	A _____ and a _____ are bigger than a _____
grape, grapefruit, tangerine	A _____ and a _____ are bigger than a _____

Be careful where you see the word "an."
Remember, an is used with a word starting with a vowel or a silent "h."

Idioms

Name: _____

Idioms are sayings which we use every day.
When your father says, **"You are driving me up the wall!"** he doesn't mean you are driving the car, he means you are making him crazy!

Try to complete the idioms below.

The answers are jumbled at the end of each line, and all the answers are **nouns** (names of things).
Write your answers on the lines.

Idiom	Meaning	Answer
1. You must play the _____.	You must play fairly	MGEA
2. She had to hold her _____.	She had to be silent	ONTUGE
3. They both bit the _____.	They both fell to the ground	UDST
4. He was all _____.	He was listening very carefully	AESR
5. Don't rub him the wrong _____.	Don't annoy him	YWA
6. Strike while the _____ is hot.	Act at once	RINO
7. She took forty _____.	She had a short sleep	NIWSK
8. Don't hit below the _____.	Don't act unfairly	EBTL
9. He turned over a new _____.	He made a new start	ELFA
10. Put your best _____ forward.	You do your best	TFOO
11. He showed his _____.	He ran away	ELHSE
12. He's down in the _____.	He's always unhappy	HMUTO
13. We threw in the _____.	We gave up trying	WELTO
14. You hit the _____ on the head.	You are exactly right	INLA
15. It's raining cats and _____.	It's raining very heavily	SDGO

Colorful Language!

Name: _____

We use **colors** in many of the common sayings we use in our daily conversations.

For example, we say someone is **in the pink** when that person is fit and healthy.

Use each of the colors listed below and place them in the correct box. Some colors are used more than once. The meanings of the phrases in **bold type** are in parentheses.

Hint: You may find these sayings in a large dictionary.

| BROWN | BLACK | WHITE | RED | BLUE | YELLOW | GREEN |

1. She was [____] **in the face** when he kissed her. (embarrassed)

2. Our team's victory was a [____] **wash**. (opponents didn't score)

3. The thieves were **caught** [____] **-handed**. (caught in the act)

4. They said he **had a** [____] **streak**. (was a coward)

5. Her garden bloomed because she **had a** [____] **thumb**. (skilled at gardening)

6. The student won a [____] **ribbon in the contest**. (first place)

7. She is a [____] **-collar worker**. (she works in an office)

8. She was **given the** [____] **light** to build a house. (given permission)

9. That theater is **a** [____] **elephant**. (costly to run and makes no profit)

10. He is **a** [____] **-collar worker**. (tradesman who works with his hands)

11. She is **the** [____] **sheep** of the family. (least respectable family member)

12. The ladies were [____] **with envy** when the prince kissed her. (jealous)

13. It was **a** [____] **-letter day** for him. (day when everything goes right)

14. She'd been **feeling** [____] all day. (feeling miserable)

Vocabulary Sleuths Book 1

Missing Numbers

Name: _____

Each of the words in the left-hand column below has a part missing, and **the missing part from the box is a number.** Look at the examples!

| TEN |ant   A person who pays rent.

| THREE |some   A group of three people.

If you think you know the answer, check its meaning in the dictionary to see if it's the same as the clue. **The clue is for the whole word!**

1. FR [ ]   Cargo moved from one place to another

2. DRIF [ ] OD   Pieces of timber cast onto the beach by waves

3. [ ] PENCE   An old English coin no longer used

4. COL [ ] L   An officer in the army

5. CA [ ]   An animal which is part of the dog family

6. H [ ] ST   He does not tell lies

7. DR [ ]   A male bee that doesn't have a sting

8. MIT [ ]   A kind of glove used in cold countries

9. DISH [ ] ST   Not to be trusted

10. H [ ]   Altitude

11. [ ] SOME   A group of three

12. C [ ]   A math shape

13. [ ] OR   A male singer with a high voice

14. ABAL [ ]   A sea creature with a shell

15. GLIS [ ]   To shine or sparkle in the light

Occupations

Name: _____
(Vocabulary extension)

The people in **bold type** in the sentences use the objects listed at the bottom of the page. Check each word in your dictionary and write it on the correct line beside the person who would use it.

1. The **blacksmith** shaped the metal on his _____.

2. An **orchestra leader** conducted with her _____.

3. His **dentist** pulled out a tooth with his _____.

4. Each **astronaut** looked through the _____.

5. Her **doctor** listened to her heart with a _____.

6. As she made a dress, the **dressmaker** used a _____.

7. The **butcher** chopped up the meat with a _____.

8. An **office worker** carried letters in her _____.

9. A **surgeon** completed the operation with a _____.

10. Their **gardener** collected leaves with a _____.

11. A **salesperson** entered the price on her _____.

12. Each **explorer** carried a small _____.

13. The **nurse** checked his patient with a _____.

14. One of the **police officers** carried a long _____.

15. Several **farmers** tried to repair a friend's _____.

cleaver
anvil
stethoscope
thimble
compass

thermometer
rake
cash register
plough
telescope

forceps
briefcase
baton
scalpel
truncheon

Your dictionary will help you!

Word Squares

Name: _____

These are word squares which you have to solve.

Look at the example on the right. **All answers are four-letter words** and spelling must be correct. Your **dictionary and a thesaurus** will help. Clues to the missing words are given around the squares.

a metal

L	E	A	D
I			A
P			R
S	I	N	K

body parts — unlit

subside

You may learn some new words!

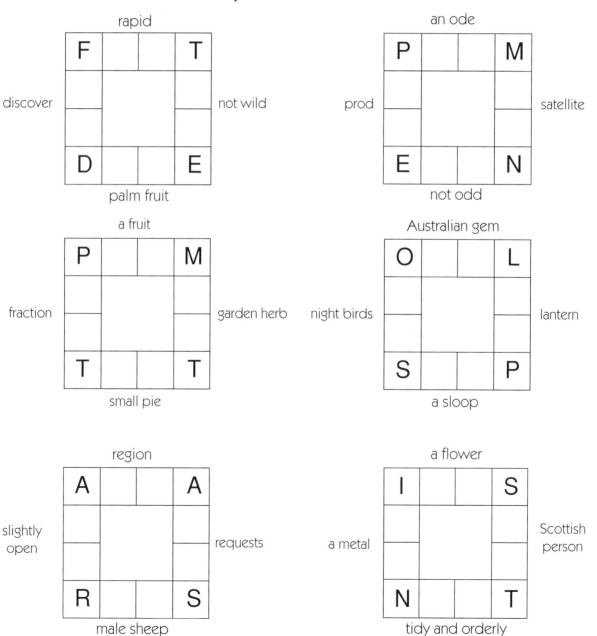

Word Target 1

Name: _____
(Dictionary work)

Follow the rules and place the words you find alongside the clues below.

T	D	R
	A	M
O	N	E
U	P	F

Rules
1. All words are four letters long.
2. The letter **T** must be in each word.
3. No names of people (e.g., Tom) or places (e.g., Texas).
4. The letter **T** can be anywhere in the word.
5. No letter is used twice in the same word.
6. There are no plurals.

Check the words in bold type in your dictionary!

1. RE____ ____   Money paid to live in a house
2. FO____ ____   A bowl in a church that holds water
3. ME____ ____   **Venison** is an example of this
4. TU____ ____   A large game and food fish
5. MO____ ____   Water-filled ditch around a castle
6. TR____ ____   A **snare** is one
7. PU____ ____   A kind of flat-bottomed boat used for leisure
8. PE____ ____   Dried **turf** used for fuel in fires
9. TO____ ____   An **amphibian** with a rough skin
10. MA____ ____   Word meaning "a friend"
11. PO____ ____   To stick out your lips when sulking
12. TA____ ____   Describes a **domesticated** animal
13. PA____ ____   The top of the head
14. DA____ ____   Pointed missile, generally thrown by hand
15. TU____ ____   A **melody**

Hint: Circle the letter Ⓣ in each word to make sure you follow the rule.

Word Target 2

Name: _____

T	I	B
	P	R
G	N	O
V	E	A

Your target is to find all the answers!
Use only the letters in the box and obey all the rules

Rules
1. The letter **T** is in all words.
2. There are no plurals.
3. No proper nouns (names of people, places).
4. No letter can be used twice in the same word.
5. Use your dictionary!

Clues

1. V___ ___T — An opening
2. TA___ ___ R — A small drum
3. P___ ___ ___T — To spin round
4. G___ ___T — A way of walking
5. TA___ ___O — A South American dance
6. PA___ ___T___ ___ — Rope used to moor a boat
7. TO___ ___ — Garment worn by ancient Romans
8. B___ ___T — A submarine is one
9. E___T — To devour
10. ___ ___ ___T — A harbor
11. ___ ___A___T — An ogre
12. ___ ___T___ — It is cast in an election
13. BO___T___ ___ — A flat straw hat
14. B___ ___T — A spoiled, impudent child
15. PO___ ___T___ ___ — A kind of hunting dog

Using the same rules, see if you can find four other words with **no fewer than four letters.**

1. _____   2. _____

3. _____   4. _____

Limericks

Name: _____
(Context clues)

Limericks are humorous (funny) poems which have **five** lines.
In a limerick, the **first**, **second** and **fifth** lines rhyme.

The **third** and **fourth** lines rhyme with each other, but with a **different** rhyme pattern from the other three lines.

The rhyming words are above each limerick.
Place them in the poems so they make sense.

---

ground   York   fork   around   cork

There was an old man from ___York___

Who tried to eat cream with a ___fork___

It splashed all ___around___

Fell down to the ___ground___

Because it wasn't kept in with a ___cork___

---

sea   jetty   bee   pretty   Betty

There was a young girl named _____

Who went for a walk on a _____

She fell into the _____

Was stung by a _____

And certainly didn't look _____

---

fainter   air   bear   painter   stare

There once was a _____

Who knew how to _____

Because he was a _____

And not a _____

He held one foot in the _____!

---

cot   insane   yacht   Spain   shot

Four men who sailed on a _____

Took a baby who slept on a _____

They sailed over to _____

Said Spaniards were _____

And left before they were _____

---

razor   Mary   fairy   laser   hairy

There once was a girl named _____

Whose face was extremely _____

She asked for a _____

But should use a _____

If she wanted to look like a _____

---

bent   tent   date   straight   Trent

There was a young man named _____

Whose nose was obviously _____

He wanted it _____

In time for a _____

So the operation was done in a _____

Adjectives

Name: _____
(Dictionary work)

Adjectives are words which describe nouns (a **tall** boy) or words which stand for nouns (he is **tall**). ("He" is a pronoun standing for the noun "boy.")
Place the correct adjective from the list into each sentence. The meaning is given in brackets. **Put the first letter of your answer in the box (☐).**

1. His writing was ☐ _____ (unreadable).
2. He crossed the ☐ _____ (waterless) desert by camel.
3. She was a very ☐ _____ (gentle) person.
4. The powerful jet flew into the ☐ _____ (blue) sky.
5. A ☐ _____ (brave) knight rescued the maiden.
6. The painter painted all the ☐ _____ (outside) walls.
7. Each ☐ _____ (broken-down) building was destroyed.
8. He plunged down the ☐ _____ (gaping) hole in the road.
9. She was more ☐ _____ (careful) than her older sister.
10. Many of the ☐ _____ (freed) prisoners were overjoyed.
11. Several stale cakes were not ☐ _____ (eatable).
12. Beware of ☐ _____ (poisonous) snakes.
13. The ☐ _____ (odd) old lady lived alone.
14. John made a ☐ _____ (quick) recovery from his illness.
15. She had a ☐ _____ (thoughtful) look on her face.
16. One stranger had long ☐ _____ (horse-like) features.
17. There's no excuse for ☐ _____ (noisy) behavior.
18. She wore a belt around her ☐ _____ (thin) waist.
19. The ☐ _____ (stubborn) donkey refused to move.
20. Many ☐ _____ (night) creatures are rarely seen.

Your word list:

slender	illegible	cautious	obstinate	yawning
ramshackle	nocturnal	rapid	meek	external
venomous	azure	valiant	edible	rowdy
equine	liberated	arid	eccentric	pensive

Now put the boxed letters into these boxes to make a sentence!

1	2	3	4	5	6	7	8	9	10	11	12	13	14	15	16	17	18	19	20

Crossword Puzzle - Similes

Name: _____

Similes are a way of making meanings clear. "Simile" comes from the Latin word *"similis,"* meaning "like." Often two unlike things are compared. For example, when you say "He is **as strong as a bull,**" you want to make it clear how strong he is so you compare him to a bull (**like** a bull).

Complete the crossword puzzle. The jumbled answers are in the brackets.

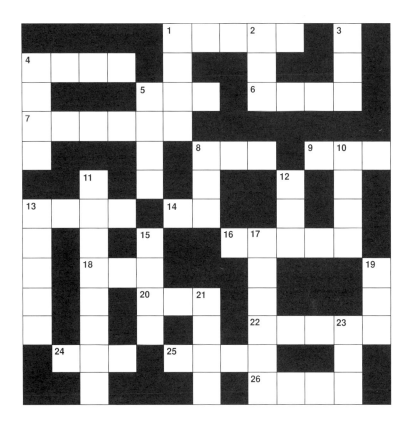

Across

1. He was as white as a ...... (hetes)
4. Her hand was as steady as a ... (kocr)
5. She was as blind as a ...... (tab)
6. She was as happy as a ...... (rkal)
7. She was as playful as a ...... (tnitke)
8. His son was as ...... as a fiddle (tfi)
9. His hand was as cold as ...... (cei)
13. The baby was as good as ...... (dlgo)
14. She was as strong as an ...... (xo)
16. He was as slow as a ...... (ilsan)
18. It was as clean as a new ...... (npi)
20. He was as wise as an ...... (low)
22. She felt as fresh as a ...... (yadsi)
24. He was as busy as an ...... (tan)
25. The girl felt as warm as ...... (olow)
26. The sum was as ...... as ABC (saye)

Down

1. She was as graceful as a ...... (wnsa)
2. The thief was as slippery as an ...... (lee)
3. The house was as old as the ...... (rak)
4. She was as thin as a ...... (kear)
5. His heart was as sound as a ...... (lelb)
8. He was as cunning as a ...... (xfo)
10. She was as black as ...... (laco)
11. It was as heavy as an ...... (tahleepn)
12. Her eyes were as blue as the ...... (ase)
13. It was as green as ...... (rgssa)
15. Her hair was as white as ...... (wosn)
17. He was as sharp as a ...... (leeend)
19. It was as bright as ...... (yda)
21. He was as brave as a ...... (noli)
23. She was as ...... as a fox (lsy)

Vocabulary Sleuths Book 1

Anagram Verbs!

Name: _____

Verbs are mainly "doing" words which show action; for example, he **ran**, she **smiled**, they **jump**.
Anagrams are words made from the jumbled letters of other words; for example, sale–seal.

Read the first sentence. You will need to rearrange the letters of the verb found in the box of the first sentence in order to complete the second sentence. If you need extra help you can refer to the answers, which are listed *out of order*, in the right column.

1. He [paled] as the strange creatures approached.

    If you [   ] hard you can reach the top of the hill.   MASTERED

2. He [wrote] several letters that morning.

    All over the city, new buildings [   ] above us.   SKIS

3. They [drove] their car to the local garage.

    The famous pirate [   ] the seas for many years.   PEELS

4. She had to [kiss] each baby for the photographs.

    David [   ] down the icy slopes every morning.   ROVED

5. Each person [said] he or she would give a prize.

    Our hospital nurse [   ] anyone who needs help.   PEDAL

6. We tried to [wrest] the money out of his hands.

    Too many visitors [   ] litter around the city's parks.   DIAL

7. [Sleep] well and then rise early for work.

    He usually [   ] off his clothes before diving in.   STRIVE

8. All of them [laid] out their presents on the table.

    They always [   ] that number, but no one answers.   TOWER

9. The students [streamed] into the auditorium.

    Each student [   ] the problems in the test.   AIDS

10. The worker [rivets] the bolts into the metal very carefully.

    You must [   ] hard to be successful.   STREW

Alliteration

Name: _____

When writers use **alliteration** they begin words with the same letters, because the words then seem to run together more smoothly and have a rhythm.

Alliteration also helps make the sayings we use easier to remember.
For example, **b**lind as a **b**at; **sp**ick and **sp**an; as **g**ood as **g**old; **th**rough **th**ick and **th**in.

Look at the example below and then make up your own alliteration sentences from the given words.

Try to make them as funny as you can!

Example:
Tiny **T**im **t**old **t**errible **t**ales **t**o **t**alkative **T**homas.

1. **M**onty **M**ouse

2. **P**eter **P**iper

3. **C**aptain **C**ook

4. The **P**ink **P**orcupine

5. **B**oys' **B**and

6. **G**eorge **G**ranite

7. **B**uffalo **B**ruce

8. **K**ing **K**ong

9. **S**amson **S**treet

10. **B**rown **B**etty

Similes – Alliteration

Name: _____

Similes are **sayings** people use all the time. We use similes when we compare somebody or something with something else so we can make very clear what we mean.

For example, if a person is very **quiet** or very **thin**, we say that person is:
- **as quiet as a mouse**; or
- **as thin as a rail**.

Some **similes** are more easily remembered because they use **alliteration**, where the main words start with the same letter.
For example, "as **b**lind as a **b**at;" "as **f**it as a **f**iddle;" "as **g**ood as **g**old."

Now try these. The answers are jumbled, but the first letter is printed in **bold** type.

1. She was as **p**retty as a _____   RIC**T**PEU

2. He said everything would be as **r**ight as _____   NI**R**A

3. The student was as **b**usy as a _____   E**B**E

4. It is late, but she is still as **b**right as a _____   TO**B**NUT

5. Each animal was as **d**ead as a _____   LON**D**OIAR

6. After the game, John was as **p**leased as _____   H**P**NUC

7. She said her brother was as **w**eak as _____   TAR**W**E

8. During summer, he was as **b**rown as a _____   E**B**RYR

9. Mary's father was as **p**roud as a _____   CEC**P**AKO

10. Even in danger, she was as **c**ool as a _____   UER**C**CBMU

11. Her story was as **d**ull as _____   TRE**D**SHIWA

12. Rik is as **m**ad as a _____ hare.   HA**M**CR

13. The monster was as **t**all as a _____   RE**T**E

14. You didn't finish because you are as **s**low as a _____   N**S**ILA

Reordering Sentences

Name: _____

The sentences below are jumbled so that they don't make sense. **Sentences should make sense**, so you have to reorder the words.

When you have placed them in the correct order, put the **last letter** of each sentence in its box to form a word reading downwards.

1. clever young the was boy very
   _____ ☐

2. under they arch both the passed
   _____ ☐

3. Hawaii only been had to he
   _____ ☐

4. two four is and seven not
   _____ ☐

5. hero had a like acted he
   _____ ☐

6. was child a given each tunic
   _____ ☐

7. to his know wanted name everybody
   _____ ☐

8. river no grew the near shrubs
   _____ ☐

9. members solo sing choir to had a
   _____ ☐

10. pieces our mirror tiny into shattered
    _____ ☐

11. time never those on boys are
    _____ ☐

12. heard all loud cries their we
    _____ ☐

The mystery word is: _____

Vocabulary Sleuths Book 1   *World Teachers Press®* 25

Jumbled Sentences

Name: _____

These sentences are all mixed up. Sentences should make sense, so you have to "unjumble" them. The first word in each correct sentence is in **bold type**, and you should learn something new from each sentence.

Put the last letter of each sentence in its box to form a word (reading downwards).

1. summer, is weather often **In** warm the.

2. polo **The** ride teams horses in.

3. express **A** is train fast an called.

4. is of **Baghdad** city Iraq capital the.

5. of in Andes the are Mountains Peru **Parts**.

6. woman **An** sari Indian a may wear.

7. in make **Governments** money mint a.

8. called is **One** Pluto the planets of.

9. are on grapes **Tasty** vine our grown.

10. bishops **Players** in and use knights chess.

Homophones

Name: _____

The word **homophone** comes from two Greek words "homos" (same) and "phone" (sound). They are words with the **same sound** but with **different spellings and meanings**.

In the sentences below, the wrong homophones, in **bold type**, have been used because they sound the same. Write the correct answers in the boxes. The jumbled answers are at the end of the line.

Examples:

Mother baked a cake with white **flower**.   flour

The king was popular throughout his **rain**.   reign

1. Elijah was a Biblical **profit**. _____ HOPRPTE
2. The angler tried to catch a **place**. _____ IPALEC
3. The musician played a tune on an ancient **loot**. _____ TLUE
4. His uncle served in the Royal Armored **Core**. _____ CPSRO
5. For her bravery, she was given a **meddle**. _____ ADLME
6. He had a mouth infection on his upper **palette**. _____ AAPLET
7. The spoiled baby began to **ball**. _____ BWLA
8. The worker climbed down the chimney **flew**. _____ ULFE
9. The **sweet** of rooms made up a small apartment. _____ UEITS
10. In the garden, she grew the herb **time**. _____ HYTEM
11. The bride walked down the **isle**. _____ IASEL
12. She sewed the thread around the **islet**. _____ TEEELY
13. In church they all sang the popular **him**. _____ YHNM
14. The wedding cake was built in **tears**. _____ ERTSI
15. The old woman carried water in a **picture**. _____ HITPCRE
16. He wore shoes of brown **swayed**. _____ USDEE
17. Each diamond weighed nine **carrots**. _____ AACSTR

Spelling must be correct!

Homonyms

Name: _____

The word **homonym** comes from the Greek *homos* (meaning "same") and *onyma* (meaning "name"). **Homonyms** have **different meanings** but are **pronounced and spelled the same**.

In the sentences below, the same homonym is used twice in each sentence, but there are clues to give you the two different meanings.

Examples:

1. The flying [BAT] landed on the handle of the cricket [BAT].
2. He held a small [PALM] tree in the [PALM] of his hand.

The correct answers are given, jumbled, at the end of the sentences.

1. A _____ built a nest on top of the huge _____.   ANRCE
2. The sailors drank _____ as they sailed into _____.   TOPR
3. The athlete decided to _____ as he caught a _____.   ARTIN
4. You can't _____ with swords near our garden _____.   NFCEE
5. The _____ cavalry officer captured the Indian _____.   VERBA
6. There was only _____ left when the _____ tree burned down.   AHS
7. He made a _____ to sell _____ to the timber mill.   LADE
8. It was _____ p.m. before the rowing _____ finished.   HIETG
9. He _____ to escape but was caught and _____ in court.   DITER
10. We learn about _____ of fish in our _____.   SOHSCOL
11. My _____ was treated at hospital by a _____.   TSSREI
12. She _____ the smooth surface of the piece of _____.   LFTE
13. He heard a noisy _____ as they played _____.   TCICEKR
14. He played with a _____ on the _____ floor.   LAMEBR
15. The stem of the _____ damaged the _____ in his eye.   RIIS

If you are not sure you have the right word, check both meanings in a dictionary!

Anagrams

Name: _____

When we jumble the letters of a word to make another word, we have made an **anagram. Team** is an anagram of **mate** because the same letters are used.

In the problems below, you have to find **two** anagrams from the given word and place them in the correct boxes. Clues are given to help you.

Look carefully at this example.

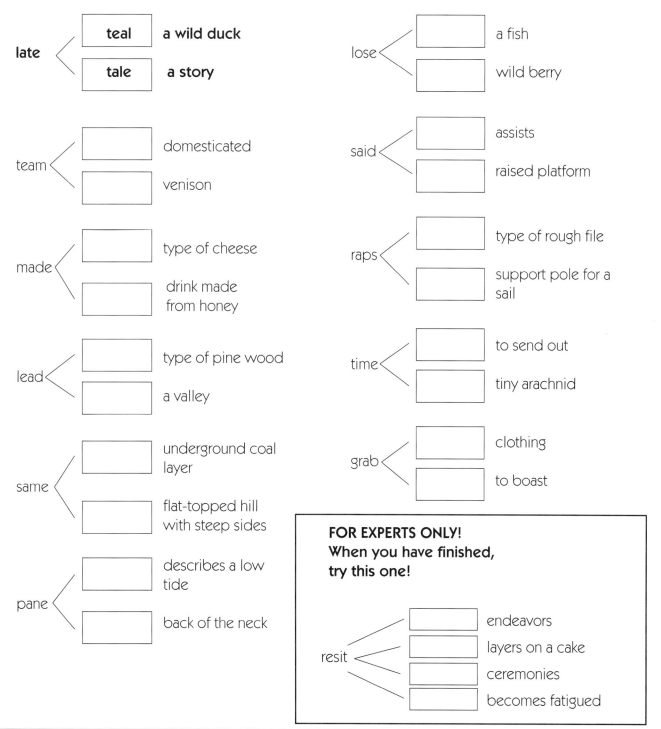

Derivations

Name: _____

Many of the words in our language come from other countries and often have interesting origins.

Try to find the missing words by using your dictionary and the clues from the information.
There is a connection between the missing word and the word in **bold type** in the information.

Word	Meaning of word	Information
W _ _ _ _ _ _ _	Twenty-four hours	After the Norse god **Woden**
P _ _ _	A sweet red wine	After the Portuguese city **Oporto**
A _ _ _ _	A book of maps	After a **titan** (a giant in Greek legend) who held the world on his shoulders
BA _ _ _ _ _ _	A cooking method	From the Spanish word **barbacoa**, which was a frame for drying meat
A _ _ _ _ _ _ _	A system of letters	From **alpha** and **beta**, the first two letters of the Greek system
BO _ _ _	A knife	After an American frontiersman
T _ _ _ _ _ _	Twenty-four hours	After **Thor**, the Norse god of war
M _ _ _ _ _ _	An insect	From the Latin **musca** (= a fly)
CH _ _ _ _ _ _ _	A tiny dog	After a state in Mexico
M _ _ _ _ _ _	A scientific instrument	After a stone from **Magnesia**
CAM _ _ _ _ _	A scented shrub	After G.J. **Kamel**, a missionary working in the far East
CE _ _ _ _ _ _	A temperature scale	After a Swedish astronomer
CA _ _ _ _ _ _ _ _	Type of coffee	From **capuchin**, the brown clothing worn by monks
TA _ _ _ _ _ _	To tease	From **Tantalus**, whom Zeus condemned to stand in water which receded every time he stooped to drink (Greek myth)

Collective Nouns

Name: _____

Collective nouns are nouns which stand for a number of people or things.
Examples:
- A **pack** wolves
- A **crowd** of people

In the sentences below, the words in **bold type** tell you what is in each collection and the collective noun itself is hidden in the sentence.
Look at the example.
Circle the noun hidden in the sentence and write it in the column.

Example:
- He ate a (bun, ch)eese and some **grapes**. (A bunch of grapes)

1. We had to flee to the **ships** in the port.   ___ ___ ___ E ___

2. They can't stay if lockers are used to keep **birds**.   ___ ___ ___ C ___

3. An organ given to him was stolen by **thieves**.   ___ ___ N ___

4. The eyes of the **puppies** glittered in the light.   ___ ___ ___ ___ E ___

5. I hear my **soldiers** have won a great victory.   ___ R ___ ___

6. Any cheap art you sell raises money for the **climbers**.   ___ ___ ___ T ___

7. We can't gag Glenda because she talks to **geese**!   ___ A ___ ___ ___ ___

8. It feels warm and that means more **insects**!   ___ ___ A ___ ___

9. She bought several cute American **horses**.   T ___ ___ ___

10. The first rib eaten by the **cannibals** was tasty!   ___ ___ ___ ___ E

11. The echo iron gongs make would drown out **singers**.   ___ ___ O ___ ___

12. He entered the crowded room full of **spectators**.   ___ ___ O ___ ___

13. She could at least afford to pay her **servants**.   ___ ___ A ___ ___

14. Peaches the cat sat on the **drawers**.   ___ ___ E ___ ___

15. The echo stopped when the **angels** finished singing.   ___ O ___ ___

You can check any collective nouns in your dictionary if you are not sure of the answer.

Adjectives

Name: _____

Adjectives are words we use to **describe** people or things.
Some adjectives we use all the time!
For example, we say "a **nice** day," "a **good** boy," or "a **great** movie."

The **adjectives** in **bold type** in the sentences are the ones we use a lot.
Use the adjectives at the bottom of the sheet and put each one on its correct line, so the **bold adjective** has the same meaning as the adjective on the line next to it.

1. They built a house on the **empty** _____ block.

2. There was a **sad** _____ expression on his face.

3. We had a **happy** _____ time at the party.

4. He was taken to a **dirty** _____ cell in the prison.

5. The **brave** _____ hunter escaped from the fierce lion.

6. She made **many** _____ attempts to escape.

7. They all agreed he was a **rich** _____ man.

8. She was the **honest** _____ person they required.

9. He was sorry he shared a tent with his **untidy** _____ friend.

10. We both saw the **huge** _____ area destroyed by bombs.

11. Her parents didn't like her **rude** _____ boyfriend.

12. The visitor was a **famous** _____ visitor from overseas.

13. They saw many **old** _____ temples on their holiday.

14. There were several **noisy** _____ passengers on the train.

15. The small orange had a **sour** _____ taste.

wealthy	mournful	grimy
bitter	impolite	trustworthy
numerous	ancient	notable
vacant	jovial	bold
boisterous	immense	slovenly

Word Pyramids

Name: _____

When your answers are completed, you will have a pyramid shape, because **each answer has one more letter than the answer above it**. Clues are given for each word. Look at the example on the right.

If you find you know an answer lower down the pyramid—then work upwards!

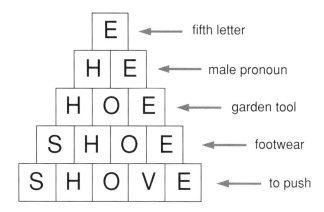

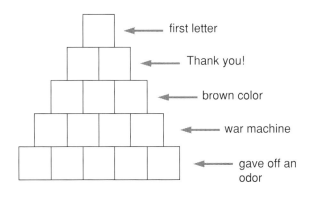

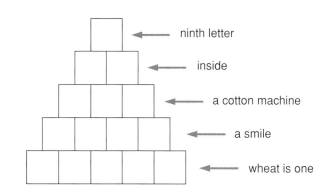

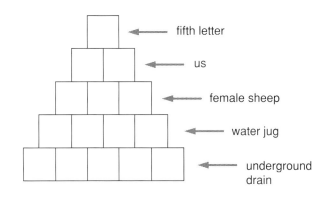

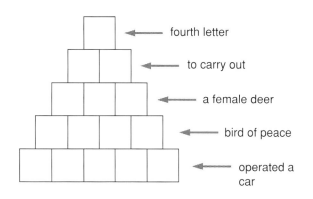

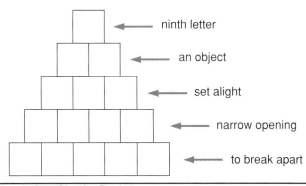

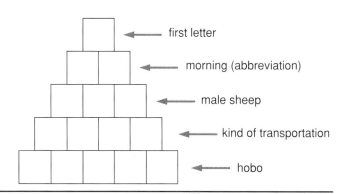

Vocabulary Sleuths Book 1 — World Teachers Press 33

Acrostic

Name: _____

After you have solved the clues across in this acrostic, you will find that you have a **capital city** in the **first column** reading downwards.

When you have discovered the name of the capital city, answer the questions below:

Using your dictionary for the **bold** words will help you!

#	Clue
1. _ _ N _ _	You would look through a **pane** here!
2. _ _ E	To clear your throat, attract attention
3. _ H _	This form of transport has a **prow**
4. _ _ _ P _ _ _	**Patients** are found in this building
5. _ _ S _	Part of your foot
6. _ T _	**Music books** have many of these
7. _ A _	This **swings** open as part of a fence
8. _ E _	There are this number of years in a **decade**
9. _ _ _ O _ _	A shape with equal opposite sides
10. _ E _	A **trawler** would use one

↙ **Your city is here!**

11. In which country is this city? _____

12. After whom was it named? _____

13. What is that person famous for? _____

_____

_____

Mis_ing Parts

Name: _____

All the **missing parts** below are the names of **living creatures**. You are given a clue for the whole word and the missing part. Look at the examples.

As you are given the first part of the whole word, you can use your dictionary. You need to check the whole word *and* the missing part to make sure you are correct. You should learn many new words!

Whole word	Whole Word Clue	Missing part clue	Answer
Examples:			
POTTER	Worker in clay	Water mammal	OTTER
WHEEL	Early invention	Sea creature	EEL
KA ___ ___ ___	Eskimo canoe	Wild ox of Tibet	YAK
SHUTTLE ___ ___ ___ ___	Used in badminton	Male bird	COCK
RIS ___ ___ ___ ___	Small pastry	A fish	SOLE
ZIGGU ___ ___ ___	Ancient temple	A rodent	RAT
WH ___ ___ ___	A sea snail	A large deer	ELK
FORE ___ ___ ___ ___ ___	Ancestors	Ursine animals	BEARS
HEAT ___ ___ ___	A pagan	A female bird	HEN
MON ___ ___ ___ ___ ___	Snake-killing animal	A large bird	GOOSE
HAR ___ ___ ___	To annoy	Wild donkey	ASS
ESC ___ ___ ___ E	A fugitive	Tailless monkey	APE
TEN ___ ___ ___	A lessee	Lives in a colony	ANT
CR ___ ___ ___	Angler's basket	Sea creature	EEL
SCA ___ ___ ___ ___	Climbing	Ocean fish	LING
BIT ___ ___ ___ ___	Wading bird	Migratory seabird	TERN
BL ___ ___ ___ ___ ___	Body organ	Venomous snake	ADDER

Spelling must be correct!

Acrostic - World Rivers

Name: _____

When you have solved each of the clues below, your answers will be famous rivers of the world.

You will then find a word reading down the first column. Use this word to complete the sentence at the bottom of the page.

				O		South American river and female warrior in Greek legend
	E					River flowing through France's capital, Paris
		G				Some of the earliest cities were near this river in Iraq
			N			Flows through some of Germany's largest cities
				C		Flows into the ocean near Trinidad
			E			Cairo and the pyramids are near this river
	R					River in the tropical part of Western Australia
		S						P		Old Man River (USA)
	B					Long Spanish river near the Pyrenees mountain range
	E					Flows into the Gulf of Mexico near New Orleans
		P				One of Papua New Guinea's largest northern rivers

My answer down the first column is _____

They are _____

_____

_____

_____

_____

36 World Teachers Press®   Vocabulary Sleuths Book 1

Crossword Puzzle - Nouns

Name: _____

A noun is a name of something or somebody.
For example, **dog, London, Peter** and **pencil** are all **nouns**.

All the answers in this crossword are nouns.

Across
3. Badly built cabin
6. Tailless monkeys
7. A seabird
9. His motto is "be prepared"
13. Used by **anglers**
15. Tiny birds
16. Tree that bears cones
17. Large member of the **feline** family
18. Young horses
20. These are **wagers**
21. A bird's beak
22. A seat in a church

Down
1. **Automobiles**
2. A **bold** person
4. This is worn on your head
5. A **sovereign**
8. A snake-like sea creature
10. An **edible** root vegetable.
11. A vase with a pedestal
12. Examinations
14. **Odors**
15. A **spouse**
19. Small poisonous snake

Hint: Using your dictionary for the meaning of the words in bold type will help you!

Fun Word Rhymes

Name: _____

This is a fun sheet, but you will learn many new words as you will need to look up the words in **bold type** in your dictionary.

Look at the example first.

Clues	Rhyming answer
Conceited waterbird	Vain crane

Now it is your turn!
Spelling must be correct!

Clues	Rhyming answers
A **corpulent** feline	A f___ ___ c___ ___
A **naked** fruit	A b___ ___ ___ p___ ___ ___
A **coy** insect	A s___ ___ f___ ___
A **wan** sea mammal	A p___ ___ ___ w___ ___ ___ ___
Pleasant **rodents**	n___ ___ ___ m___ ___ ___
A **beige** fool	A b___ ___ ___ c___ ___ ___ ___
A **drab** steer	A d___ ___ ___ b___ ___ ___
An **opulent** warlock	A r___ ___ w___ ___ ___ ___
A **frigid** nincompoop	A c___ ___ ___ f___ ___ ___
An **inane** flower	A s___ ___ ___ ___ l___ ___ ___
A **jovial** fruit	A m___ ___ ___ c___ ___ ___ ___
A **jocular** canine	A j___ ___ ___ c___ ___ ___ ___
A **plump** fish	A s___ ___ ___ t___ ___ ___ ___
A **hirsute** bird	A h___ ___ ___ c___ ___ ___ ___
An **acute** musical instrument	A s___ ___ ___ ___ h___ ___ ___

Now make up your own example and see if the class can solve it!

Word Snake - Social Studies

Name: _____

The answers to this problem are all connected and wind like a snake.
Remember: The **last letter** of one answer gives you the **first letter** of the answer which follows it.

Clues:

1. Capital city of Peru. _____

2. You would see the Parthenon on the Acropolis in this capital city of Greece. _____

3. The world's largest desert. _____

4. An American state sold by Russia to America. _____

5. South American mountain range. _____

6. Long English river flowing into the Bristol Channel. _____

7. Fiords are found in this country. _____

8. Scene of war between Serbs and Croats. _____

9. Ocean in the northern hemisphere. _____

10. The pyramids are built near this city. _____

11. The gods of Greek legend lived on this mountain. _____

12. The world famous Edinburgh Festival is held in this country. _____

13. The famous white cliffs are near this English city on the south coast. _____

14. Traditionally you would throw coins into this city's Trevi fountain. _____

15. Famous statues of unknown origin are seen on this island in the south Pacific Ocean. _____

"Let's go, man!"

Name: _____
(Dictionary work)

Place the words at the bottom of the page into the correct sentence.

All words begin with **man**, and there are clues in the sentences to help you.

1. The _____ was the fiercest monkey he had faced.
2. He played a new tune on his _____.
3. Some _____ trees blocked our way through the swamp.
4. A detective clamped the _____ on the thief's wrists.
5. A large _____ was feeding on plants in tropical waters.
6. The Chinese _____ allowed other officials to enter.
7. His lower _____ was broken in the fight.
8. _____ is a metal mixed with other metals to form an alloy.
9. The horse ate hay from a large wooden _____.
10. The Spanish girl wore a _____ over her head and shoulders.
11. Her hands were given a _____ by the beautician.
12. The attractive _____ modeled the new clothes.
13. The visitors admired the furniture in the huge _____.
14. The _____ sailed into the harbor with guns blazing.
15. Each old _____ had been written by hand.
16. He liked the _____ better than any other tropical fruit.
17. The army _____ was planned by their top generals.
18. He didn't intend to kill his friend, so he was tried for _____.
19. He used the driver's _____ to learn all about his new car.
20. Some American Indians believe in a spirit called a _____.

Choose from these words:

maneuver	manual	manacles	manatee
manger	mantilla	mannequin	mandrill
man-of-war	manicure	manganese	mandible
mangrove	mandarin	mango	manuscript
mandolin	manitou	manslaughter	mansion

Creatures and Their Homes

Name: _____

Human beings live in chalets, mansions, cottages, palaces etc., all names for different kinds of dwellings.

Find the homes of the creatures in the word search and place them into the correct sentences below.

t	l	s	p	e	o	s	h	p	y
s	h	e	n	t	c	o	t	e	d
h	u	t	c	h	o	p	x	n	r
l	o	t	o	p	o	l	w	h	e
o	l	e	l	a	p	i	a	r	y
d	v	h	o	l	a	i	r	t	n
g	m	e	n	a	g	e	r	i	e
e	n	e	y	r	i	e	e	p	o
t	s	f	p	m	o	u	n	d	s
e	a	r	t	h	n	y	s	l	e

1. An eagle's nest high in the mountains is an [_ | y | _ | i | _].
2. A burrowing animal raises its young in an [_ | a | _ | t | _].
3. All the doves flew back to the [c | _ | t | _] at night.
4. A squirrel makes its home in a [_ | r | _ | y].
5. A [_ | u | _ | c | _] is where we keep tame rabbits.
6. A bear may hibernate in its [_ | a | _ | r] for the winter.
7. There are thousands of ants in a [_ | o | _ | o | _ | y].
8. Tigers were kept in a [_ | e | _ | g | _ | r | _] for the public to see.
9. Wild rabbits live in underground tunnels called [_ | a | _ | r | _ | n | _].
10. The badger comes out of its [_ | e | _] at night to hunt.
11. Beavers live in a [_ | o | _ | g | _] they build in a lake or stream.
12. Bees kept for their honey are found in an [_ | p | _ | a | _ | y].
13. Anteaters break open [_ | o | _ | n | _ | s] to eat the termites inside.
14. A fox had attacked the poultry in the hen [_ | o | _ | p].
15. His sheep were kept in a [_ | _ | n] during icy weather.

Vocabulary Sleuths Book 1

Collective Nouns

Name: _____

A collective noun is a noun which stands for a collection of things, even when it is in its singular form (e.g. a flock of sheep).

Find them in the word search and place them into the correct sentences.

t	n	s	o	p	s	w	a	r	m
c	l	n	s	c	h	o	o	l	s
l	y	s	e	t	o	l	o	z	h
u	b	r	i	g	a	d	e	s	a
m	o	t	x	f	l	e	e	t	n
p	u	n	n	e	t	h	e	r	d
e	q	l	w	s	n	o	b	o	t
s	u	i	t	e	l	s	e	u	x
t	e	a	m	s	o	t	n	p	o
o	t	n	x	l	i	t	t	e	r

1. The star of the show was given a [_ | o | u | _ | u | e | _] of flowers.
2. This [_ | u | _ | e | _] of strawberries was not expensive.
3. We could see the [_ | _ | o | a | _] of fish.
4. The general saluted the [_ | _ | i | _ | a | _ | e] of troops as they passed.
5. A huge [_ | _ | e | e | _] of ships dotted the harbor.
6. They both decided to buy the [_ | u | i | _] of furniture.
7. Any [_ | _ | a | _ | m] of bees can be dangerous so be careful.
8. A [_ | _ | o | o | _] of whales was stranded on the beach.
9. Several boys were hiding behind a [_ | _ | u | _ | p] of trees.
10. We saw a marvelous [_ | _ | o | u | _ | e] of dancers at the festival.
11. I chose a pet from the [_ | i | _ | _ | e | _] of pups.
12. Across the plains thundered a [_ | e | _] of antelopes.
13. She plucked a [_ | a | _] of bananas from the tree.
14. The painting showed a [_ | o | _] of adoring angels.
15. He couldn't control the [_ | e | a | _] of horses.

Oceans and Continents

Name: _____

Your answers are found in the oceans or continents of the world.

Highlight them in your word search and then place them against the correct clues below.

You may need your atlas to find or check some of your answers.

s	p	a	c	i	f	i	c	b	t
r	e	n	c	o	o	k	v	o	s
i	n	d	e	a	s	t	e	r	u
l	g	e	g	o	b	i	n	e	p
a	u	s	t	r	a	l	i	a	e
n	i	p	a	r	i	s	c	a	r
k	n	i	l	e	o	o	e	u	i
a	s	o	u	t	h	e	r	n	o
o	a	l	a	s	k	a	e	e	r
t	e	s	t	h	e	l	e	n	a

1. Deepest and largest ocean in the world.
   [ ][a][ ][i][ ][i][ ]

2. This is a huge island which is also a continent.
   [ ][ ][ ][ ][a][ ][i][a]

3. Largest lake on the North American continent.
   [ ][u][ ][e][ ][i][o]

4. Pacific Ocean island named after an explorer.
   [ ][o][ ][o]

5. Desert in the continent of Asia.
   [ ][o][ ][i]

6. The nearest ocean to the continent of Antarctica.
   [ ][o][u][ ][ ][e][ ][ ]

7. Pacific Ocean island where ancient stone statues are found.
   [ ][a][ ][ ][e][ ]

8. You'd travel along city streets in boats in this city in the continent of Europe.
   [ ][e][ ][i][ ][e]

9. The Arctic Ocean washes the north coast of this American state.
   [ ][ ][a][ ][ ][a]

10. Long mountain range in the South American continent. [ ][n][ ][e][ ]

11. This river, the world's longest, is on the continent of Africa. [ ][i][ ][e]

12. Napoleon was imprisoned on this island in the Atlantic Ocean.
    [ ][ ].[ ][e][ ][e][ ][a]

13. This Indian Ocean island was once called Ceylon. [ ][ ][i][ ][a][ ][a]

14. The Eiffel Tower can be seen in this city on the continent of Europe. [ ][a][ ][i][ ]

Endangered Animals

Name: _____

t	e	l	p	h	o	h	e	b	t	w
w	l	x	z	l	t	e	n	o	e	x
b	e	a	r	b	a	d	g	e	r	j
f	p	a	n	d	a	g	x	t	w	a
r	h	i	n	o	c	e	r	o	s	g
y	a	n	o	t	n	h	k	l	b	u
t	n	b	x	t	w	o	o	x	i	a
o	t	i	g	e	r	g	a	y	s	r
x	n	g	o	r	i	l	l	a	o	z
l	e	o	p	a	r	d	a	k	n	b
l	b	w	d	u	g	o	n	g	w	t

Animals are threatened with extinction through hunting, superstitions (for example, powdered rhino horn is believed to have magical properties in Asia), pesticide pollution, introduced predators and destruction of their natural habitat.

Highlight the animals in the word search and then place them into the clues.

1. Early sailors thought it was a mermaid. [ ] [u] [ ] [o] [ ] [g]
2. Wild Asian ox seen by Marco Polo. [ ] [a] [ ]
3. Small animal endangered by chlamydia disease. [ ] [o] [a] [ ] [a]
4. Its horn is powdered in Asian medicines. [ ] [ ] [i] [ ] [o] [ ] [e] [ ] [o]
5. Fierce African animal of the cat family, killed for its beautiful coat. [ ] [e] [ ] [ ] [a] [ ] [ ]
6. Water mammal with webbed feet. [o] [ ] [ ] [e] [ ]
7. Yellow and black South American cat. [ ] [a] [ ] [u] [a] [ ]
8. Large animal killed for its tusks. [e] [ ] [e] [ ] [a] [ ]
9. American buffalo slaughtered by early settlers. [ ] [i] [ ] [o] [ ]
10. Once hunted for its warm fur. [ ] [e] [a] [ ]
11. Beautiful, large, striped cat. [ ] [i] [ ] [e] [ ]
12. Large burrowing animal with strong claws. [ ] [a] [ ] [ ] [e] [ ]
13. The biggest and strongest ape. [ ] [o] [ ] [i] [ ] [a]
14. Spiky, slow-moving animal often run over by cars. [ ] [e] [ ] [ ] [e] [ ] [o] [ ]
15. Large, gentle Asian animal which likes eating bamboo shoots. [ ] [a] [ ] [ ] [a]

Interesting Words

Name: _____

List below any new and interesting words you have come across while doing the activities in this book. Try to explain their meaning in your own words.

Word	Meaning

Answers

Page 6
1. elms 2. pelt 3. nest 4. lung 5. pail
6. hymn 7. crow 8. pork 9. harp

Page 7
1. gnat 2. peak 3. reed 4. ford
5. chef 6. tent

Page 8
heron; bowls; cedar; Paris
beret; moose; eland; pansy
otter; skate; camel; brass

Page 9
trick, brick, stick, sick, pick, quick
night, light, fight, slight, might, right
drain, pain, brain, train, grain, rain
brake, snake, lake, quake, rake, drake

Page 10
Prefixes
1. tripod 2. trilogy 3. tricycle
4. trident 5. trisect 6. tricolor
7. triangle 8. trireme 9. triplets
10. trimaran
Suffixes
1. adorable 2. visible 3. ignoble
4. dirigible 5. legible
6. peaceable 7. audible 8. edible
9. noticeable 10. irascible
11. changeable 12. malleable

Page 11
1. elephant, horse, mouse
2. goat, zebra, squirrel
3. mansion, palace, cabin
4. city, town, hamlet
5. ogre, titan, pygmy
6. glacier, iceberg, icicle
7. bouquet, wreath, flower
8. goose, swan, wren
9. sapling, seedling, seed
10. gnat, locust, flea
11. dolphin, herring, sardine
12. apricot, peach, grape
13. albatross, pelican, robin
14. cardigan, cloak, beret
15. grapefruit, tangerine, grape

Page 12
game; tongue; dust; ears; way; iron;
winks; belt; leaf; foot; heels; mouth;
towel; nail; dogs

Page 13
1. red 2. white 3. red 4. yellow
5. green 6. blue
7. white 8. green 9. white
10. blue 11. black 12. green
13. red 14. blue

Page 14
1. freight-eight 2. driftwood-two
3. sixpence-six 4. colonel-one
5. canine-nine 6. tench-ten
7. drone-one 8. mitten-ten
9. dishonest-one 10. height-eight
11. threesome-three
12. cone-one 13. tenor-ten
14. abalone-one 15. glisten-ten

Page 15
1. anvil 2. baton 3. forceps
4. telescope 5. stethoscope
6. thimble 7. cleaver
8. briefcase 9. scalpel 10. rake
11. cash register 12. compass
13. thermometer 14. truncheon
15. plough

Page 16
Across	Down
fast, date	find, tame
poem, even	poke, moon
plum, tart	part, mint
opal, ship	owls, lamp
area, rams	ajar, asks
iris, neat	iron, Scot

Page 17
1. rent 2. font 3. meat 4. tuna
5. moat 6. trap 7. punt 8. peat
9. toad 10. mate 11. pout 12. tame
13. pate 14. dart 15. tune

Page 18
1. vent 2. tabor 3. pivot 4. gait
5. tango 6. painter 7. toga 8. boat
9. eat 10. port 11. giant 12. vote
13. boater 14. brat 15. pointer

Page 19
York, fork, around, ground, cork
bear, stare, painter, fainter, air
bear, stare, sing, ring, air
yacht, cot, Spain, insane, shot
Mary, hairy, razor, laser, fairy
Trent, bent, straight, date, tent

Page 20
1. illegible 2. arid 3. meek 4. azure
5. valiant 6. external 7. ramshackle
8. yawning 9. cautious 10. liberated
11. edible 12. venomous
13. eccentric 14. rapid 15. pensive
16. equine 17. rowdy 18. slender
19. obstinate 20. nocturnal
I am a very clever person.

Page 21

Page 22
1. pedal 2. tower 3. roved 4. skis
5. aids 6. strew 7. peels 8. dial
9. mastered 10. strive

Page 23
Answers will vary

Page 24
1. picture 2. rain 3. bee 4. button
5. doornail 6. punch 7. water
8. berry 9. peacock 10. cucumber
11. dishwater 12. March 13. tree
14. snail

Page 25
1. The young boy was very clever.
2. They both passed under the arch.
3. He had only been to Hawaii.
4. Two and four is not seven.
5. He acted like a hero.
6. Each child was given a tunic.
7. Everybody wanted to know his name.
8. No shrubs grew near the river.
9. Choir members had to sing a solo.

Answers

10. Our mirror shattered into tiny pieces.
11. Those boys are never on time.
12. We all heard their loud cries.

The word formed is "RHINOCEROSES"

Page 26
1. In summer, the weather is often warm.
2. The teams ride horses in polo.
3. A fast train is called an express.
4. Baghdad is the capital city of Iraq.
5. Parts of the Andes Mountains are in Peru.
6. An Indian woman may wear a sari.
7. Governments make money in a mint.
8. One of the planets is called Pluto.
9. Tasty grapes are grown on our vine.
10. Players use bishops and knights in chess.

The word formed is "MOSQUITOES"

Page 27
1. prophet 2. plaice 3. lute
4. corps 5. medal 6. palate
7. bawl 8. flue 9. suite 10. thyme
11. aisle 12. eyelet 13. hymn 14. tiers
15. pitcher 16. suede 17. carats

Page 28
1. crane 2. port 3. train 4. fence
5. brave 6. ash 7. deal 8. eight 9. tried
10. schools 11. sister 12. felt
13. cricket 14. marble 15. iris

Page 29
tame; meat   edam; mead
deal; dale   seam; mesa
neap; nape   sole; sloe
aids; dais   rasp; spar
emit; mite   garb; brag
For experts: tries; tiers; rites; tires

Page 30
Wednesday; port; atlas; barbecue; alphabet; bowie; Thursday; mosquito; chihuahua; magnet; camellia; Celsius; cappuccino; tantalize

Page 31
1. fleet 2. flock 3. gang 4. litter
5. army 6. party 7. gaggle 8. swarm
9. team 10. tribe 11. choir
12. crowd 13. staff 14. chest
15. host

Page 32
1. vacant 2. mournful 3. jovial
4. grimy 5. bold 6. numerous
7. wealthy 8. trustworthy
9. slovenly 10. immense
11. impolite 12. notable
13. ancient 14. boisterous
15. bitter

Page 33
a, ta, tan, tank, stank
i, in, gin, grin, grain
e, we, ewe, ewer, sewer
d, do, doe, dove, drove
i, it, lit, slit, split
a, a.m., ram, tram, tramp

Page 34
1. window 2. ahem 3. ship
4. hospital 5. instep 6. notes
7. gate 8. ten 9. oblong 10. net
The city is Washington
11. USA 12. George Washington
13. First President USA

Page 35
yak; cock; sole; rat; elk; bears; hen; goose; ass; ape; ant; eel; ling; tern; adder.

Page 36
Amazon; Seine; Tigris; Rhine; Orinoco; Nile; Ord; Mississippi; Ebro; Red; Sepik
Extra word is "astronomers"

Page 37

Page 38
fat cat   bare pear
shy fly   pale whale
nice mice   brown clown
dull bull   rich witch
cool fool   silly lily
merry cherry   jolly collie
stout trout   hairy canary
sharp harp

Page 39
1. Lima 2. Athens 3. Sahara
4. Alaska 5. Andes 6. Severn
7. Norway 8. Yugoslavia 9. Arctic
10. Cairo 11. Olympus 12. Scotland
13. Dover 14. Rome 15. Easter

Page 40
1. mandrill   2. mandolin
3. mangrove   4. manacles
5. manatee   6. mandarin
7. mandible   8. manganese
9. manger   10. mantilla
11. manicure   12. mannequin
13. mansion   14. man-of-war
15. manuscript   16. mango
17. maneuver   18. manslaughter
19. manual   20. manitou

Page 41
1. eyrie 2. earth 3. cote 4. drey
5. hutch 6. lair 7. colony
8. menagerie 9. warrens 10. set
11. lodge 12. apiary 13. mounds
14. coop 15. pen

Answers

Page 42
1. bouquet 2. punnet 3. shoal
4. brigade 5. fleet 6. suite
7. swarm 8. school 9. clump
10. troupe 11. litter 12. herd
13. hand 14. host 15. team

Page 43
1. Pacific 2. Australia 3. Superior
4. Cook 5. Gobi 6. Southern
7. Easter 8. Venice 9. Alaska
10. Andes 11. Nile 12. St. Helena
13. Sri Lanka 14. Paris

Page 44
1. dugong 2. yak 3. koala
4. rhinoceros 5. leopard 6. otter
7. jaguar 8. elephant 9. bison
10. bear 11. tiger 12. badger
13. gorilla 14. hedgehog 15. panda

Page 45
Teacher check